The subject matter and vocabulary have been selected with expert assistance, and the brief and simple text is printed in large, clear type.

Children's questions are anticipated and facts presented in a logical sequence. Where possible, the books show what happened in the past and what is relevant today.

Special artwork has been commissioned to set a standard rarely seen in books for this reading age and at this price.

Full-colour illustrations are on all 48 pages to give maximum impact and provide the extra enrichment that is the aim of all Ladybird Leaders.

INDEX

For teachers' use, a map and geographical index is given at the back of the book.

A Ladybird Leader

big animals

written and illustrated by John Leigh-Pemberton

Publishers: Ladybird Books Ltd . Loughborough

Printed in England

The biggest animals

The biggest animal in the world is the blue whale.

It lives in the sea.

It is very rare.

The biggest animal on land is the African elephant.

The blue whale can be 100 feet (30.5 m) long and weigh 100 tons (101.6 tonnes). Its tongue alone weighs as much as an elephant.

The male (bull) African elephant weighs up to six tonnes.

It is about 11 feet (3.4 m) high at the shoulder.

The female (cow) is smaller.

Young elephants

Baby elephants are born with a thin covering of hair. This becomes thinner as the elephant grows up.

The Indian elephant

Indian elephants are smaller than African elephants.

They have smaller ears.

Their backs have a hump.

Trunks

An elephant's trunk
is just a very long nose.

It can be used for
drinking and feeding.

It can be used for
pulling down a tree
or for picking up
a pea-nut.

It can be used
for fighting.

An elephant uses the tip of its trunk almost like we use a hand.

Indian elephant (one 'finger')

African elephant (two 'fingers')

Feet

Elephants have very large, round feet.
Each foot has five toes,
but not all of them have nails.
The underneath of the foot
forms a large pad.

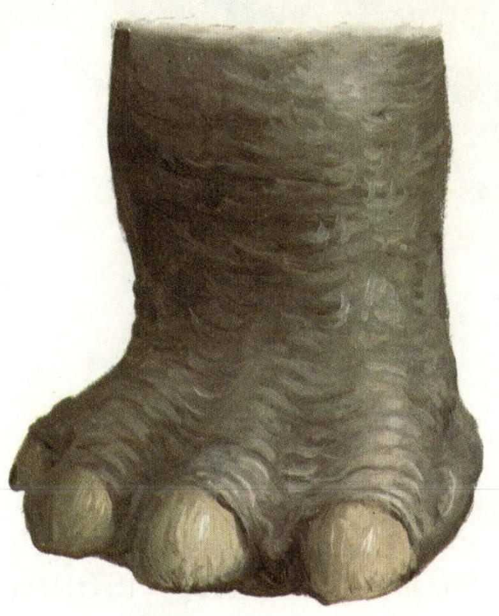

The shoulder height of an elephant
is equal to twice the measurement
round the front foot.

Skin – and keeping cool

African elephant bathing

The skin of elephants is thick and wrinkled.

They must protect themselves from the heat and insects.

To do this, they use their trunks to spray themselves with water, sand or mud.

Ears — and other senses

The ears of an African elephant

Elephants do not have good eyesight.
Their sense of smell is very good.
So is their sense of hearing.
They flap their huge ears
to cool themselves.

Tusks

Tusks are made of ivory.
They can be 10 feet (3 m) long and weigh 100 lbs. (45 kg).

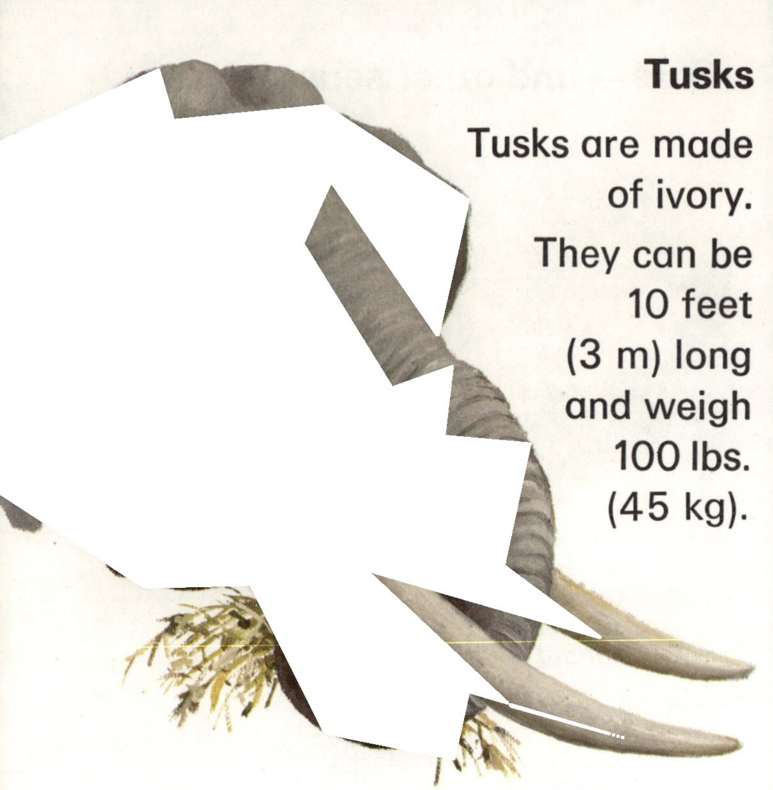

An elephant's tusks
are just two extra-large teeth.
They keep on growing
all through the elephant's life.
They are used mostly for digging,
especially for water.

Work

The Indian elephant carries his passengers in a 'howdah'.

The driver is called a 'Mahout'.

Both African and Indian elephants are used for work.

They are slow, but very strong.

They learn to move heavy loads such as tree trunks.

In India, people ride on elephants.

Where do elephants live?

Elephants live for about seventy years.
They live in jungles, forests
and grassy plains.
They form herds of about twenty,
led by an old female.

What do elephants eat?

The herds search for food nearly all day long.

They eat grass, leaves and fruit.

Every day, each elephant eats about 300 lbs. (136 kg) of food and drinks forty gallons (181 litres) of water.

The great Indian rhinoceros

These one-horned rhinos
are found only in northern India.
They inhabit jungle, grassland
or reed-beds, always near water.
They like to wallow in mud.

These huge animals can weigh
more than two tonnes.

They can be 6 feet (1.8 m) high
at the shoulder.

For most of their lives,
rhinos live alone.

The white rhino

The white rhino is the next biggest animal to the elephant.

It lives in Africa.

It can weigh three tonnes and has two horns.

The front one is very long.

This rhino eats grass.

To help it to do this,
it has a straight mouth.

The black rhino (see next page)
eats leaves and twigs, so it has a
pointed upper lip.

Black rhinos

Black rhinos live in Africa.
They are smaller than white rhinos.
They have rounder ears
and a pointed upper lip.
They are 'browsers' —
meaning they eat leaves and twigs.

Black rhinos can be more than
5 feet (1.5 m) high at the shoulder.

Although so big, they can gallop
at 28 miles (45 kilometres) per hour.

They are the most dangerous
of all the rhinos.

Two rare rhinos

The Javan rhino is like a small Indian rhino.

There are just a few left — mostly in Java.

The Sumatran rhino is the size of a pony.

It is the only rhino with hair.

Rhino's horns and feet

Rhino horn is made of the same stuff as our finger nails.

This is matted together to form a hard lump.

Some kinds of rhino have two horns. Others have only one.

All rhinos have three toes on each foot.

Skin

The skin of rhinos is thick and wrinkled.

It is arranged in folds.

Rhinos like to bathe and to wallow in mud or dust.

This helps to protect them from insects.

Charging

Most rhinos are quiet
and rather timid animals.

All of them are dangerous
if frightened or wounded.

If a smell or sound scares them,
they will charge towards it.

Two kinds of hippo live in Africa.
The big hippo lives in rivers.
The rare pygmy hippo lives alone
in wet forests.

Hippopotamus

Big hippos live in small groups.

A fully-grown male
can be 5 feet (1.5 m) tall
at the shoulder.

He can weigh four tonnes.

The females are smaller.

The big hippo's day—

During the day,
hippos lie in the water.
When they float,
their noses, eyes and ears
are just above the water.
They often sleep while floating.

—and night

At night, hippos come ashore
to eat grass.

To find it,
they travel up to twenty miles
(32 kilometres) in a night.

They always stay close
to the water.

The river bed

Hippos are good divers and swimmers.
They can stay under water
for about five minutes.
Sometimes they stay even longer.
They can walk on the river bed.

Baby hippos

Hippos have one baby at a time.

These are known as calves,
and are born under water.

They are fed in the water.

They can swim before they can walk.

The hippo's mouth

Hippos use their lips and teeth to crop the grass.

In one night, a hippo may eat 150 lbs. (68 kg) of grass.

The long, sharp teeth in the bottom jaw are used for fighting.

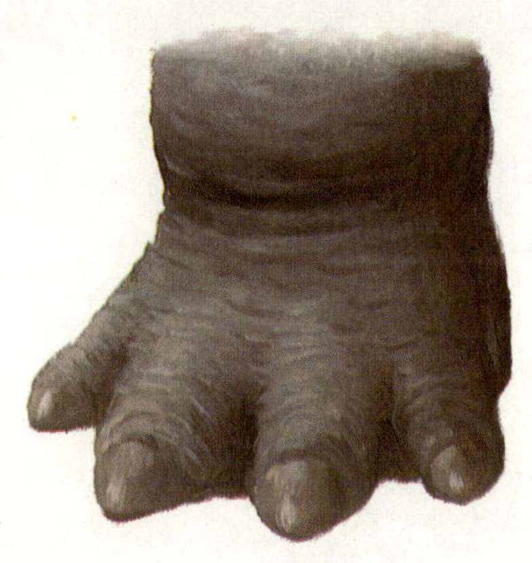

Hippo's feet and skin

Hippos have four toes on each foot.
There is a nail like a small hoof
on each toe.
The skin of hippos
contains a red, oily liquid.
This protects the skin
from water and heat.

Giraffes

Giraffes are the tallest of all land animals.

A fully-grown male can be 18 feet (5.5 m) tall.

Giraffes live on the grass plains of Africa.

The giraffe's long neck
has seven bones.
The human neck
is much shorter
but has
the same number.

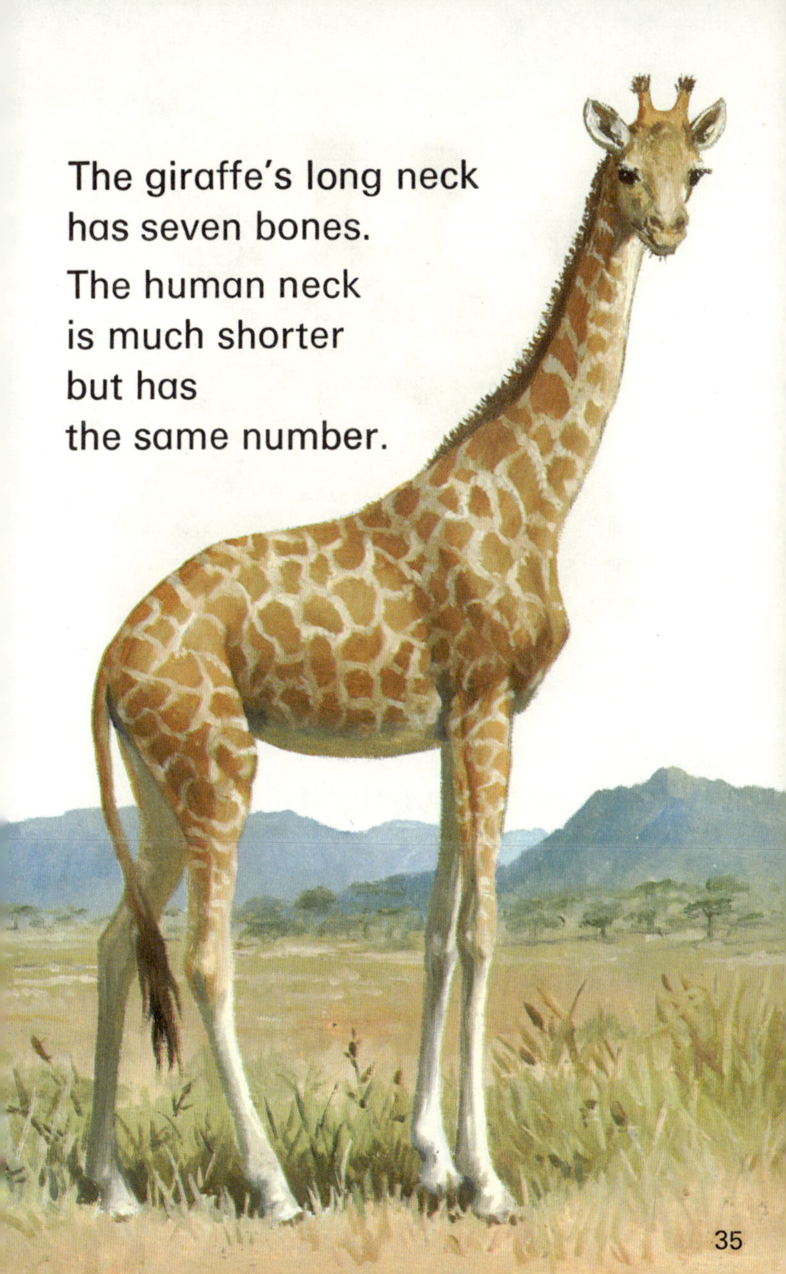

The giraffe's eyesight

Most big animals have poor eyesight, but the giraffe can see for miles. This helps to keep it safe from enemies, such as lions.

Eating and drinking

Giraffes feed mostly on the leaves of trees.

Their long necks help them to gather food which other animals cannot reach.

When they drink, they have to stretch their front legs out sideways.

Camels

For thousands of years,
camels have been used by man.
They carry heavy loads
or are used for riding.

The Bactrian camel lives in the cold deserts of Asia.

It has two humps and a thick, woolly coat.

This big animal is 7 feet (2 m) high at the shoulder.

There are just a few wild ones left in Mongolia.

All the others are tame animals.

The Arabian camel

The Arabian camel has one hump. It lives in the hot deserts of North Africa.

Man has taken it to work in other places such as Asia, Australia, America and in the southern parts of Europe.

There are no wild Arabian camels left.

The camel's food

Camels eat very coarse leaves or grasses.

They can go for a long time without drinking.

The camel's hump

A camel's hump is a store of food.

It is made of fat.

A camel can live on this
for a long time.

The longer a camel goes without food
the smaller the hump gets.

The camel's eyes, nose and feet

Camels must be able
to protect themselves
against sand and snow storms.
So they have thick eye-lashes.
They can close their nostrils.
They have broad, padded feet.

The moose — the largest deer

In America, this animal is called a moose.

In Europe, it is called an elk.

A male moose can be 7 feet (2 m) high at the shoulder.

It can weigh about 1,874 lbs. (850 kg).

The eland — the largest antelope

Elands live in Africa.

The biggest are 6 feet (1.8 m) high at the shoulder.

They can weigh about 1,984 lbs. (900 kg).

Although it is so heavy, this animal can easily jump a fence 6 feet (1.8 m) high.

The largest European animal
is the wisent
or European bison. *(right)*

There are only
a few left.

They live in Poland
and in Russia.

The wisent lives in forests
and eats leaves and grass.

The largest American animal
is the bison or buffalo. *(left)*

It is 6 feet (1.8 m) high at the shoulder
and weighs one tonne.

This animal lives on the prairie
and eats grass.

The gaur — the largest ox

The gaur belongs to the same family as our farm cattle.
It lives in forests in Asia.
('Gaur' rhymes with 'sour')

A big bull gaur
is almost 7 feet (2 m) high
from the ground to the top of his hump.

The argali — the largest sheep

This shy mountain animal
lives in the cold parts of China
and Siberia.

There is a smaller wild sheep like it
in Canada and the U.S.A.

It is called the bighorn sheep.

An argali is about 4 feet (1.2 m) high
at the shoulder.

The horns can be 6 feet (1.8 m) long.

The largest Australian animal

Many large animals
like the camel and the buffalo
have been brought to Australia.

These are not really
true Australian animals.

Kangaroos can jump 9 feet (2.7 m) high and 30 feet (9 m) in distance

The largest, truly Australian animal
is the red kangaroo.

Standing up, it is 6 feet (1.8 m) tall.

The Kodiak bear

The largest, flesh-eating animal
is a giant kind of brown bear.
It lives in the Kodiak islands
near Alaska.

Kodiak bears weigh threequarters of a tonne

The polar bear is bigger.
It lives in the sea and on ice,
not on land.

Map of the world, showing where anim